A Step by Step

Guide to

utting, Perming and Highlighting

Children's Hair

Written and illustrated
by

Laurie Punches

Published by Punches Production
South Lake Tahoe California

Published by Punches Productions
South Lake Tahoe California
Manufactured in the United States
of America.

Punches, Laurie C.
How to Simply Cut Hair for Children
"A Punches Productions Book."

Publisher's Cataloging in Publication Data
1. Haircutting

1 2 3 4 5 6 7 8 9 10

Library of Congress Catalog Number
89-090694
ISBN 0-929883-10-1

Acknowledgments

The author would like to acknowledge the help and support of Jack Rogers and Mark Rayburn for layout, design and production, Carla Martinez for editing, Steve Björkman for the cover illustration and Virgil Masalta for the author's photograph.

Dedication

This book is dedicated to my husband companion and best friend Pete, and our four beautiful children Ryan, Katie, Michael and Jeffrey.

I love you!

Disclaimer

This book in no way claims to be a substitute for beauty school. It is merely a haircutting guide for the non-professional to be used in the home. Any product containing manufacturer's directions should be followed and used as the manufacturer intended. **This book then becomes a secondary reference to the manufacturers instructions.**

Table of Contents

Foreword

With the early age fashion consciousness through media and peer group... designer clothes at preschool age that cost more than your own (for one-fifth of the material)... and hair salon prices on the rise who can afford monthly haircuts for the entire family? Most mothers wonder if there will be any money left in the monthly budget to even have her own hair done.

Parents wonder where they can get an <u>economical</u>, yet <u>quality</u> children's haircut <u>NOW</u>...**(without a half-hour wait)**? Moms are often faced with trying situations throughout the day...(especially in public places such as shops, restaurants, and beauty salons)... where some people think children should be seen... <u>but</u> not heard... even if it's happy noise!? The reality is that even the most well behaved children will be "children" no matter where they are. The tension to comform to public etiquette can often be enough to cause mothers to choose the easier and less stressful solution of "just staying at home".

This book was designed to create a desirable alternative. Even if you have no knowledge or experience cutting children's hair, this book can teach you how to cut just about any child's hair. This step by step haircutting guide to **the six basic haircuts** can be used for all types of hair whether long, short, thick, fine, straight or curly. Haircutting for girls and boys is identical, the only variables being length and angles. Exploration is part of the adventure. Most of all just relax and have fun!

Fashions and styles will keep on changing, but basic haircutting always stays the same.

Introduction

Four ingredients are needed to successfully cut hair. The first ingredient is to have a strong **desire to learn.** This desire may be to save money by stretching the time between haircuts, cut family and friend's hair or just for fun.

The second ingredient is to have **a knowledge of haircutting** which this book will provide.

The third ingredient is to gain **confidence** which comes naturally with understanding basic haircutting. Confidence grows with experience.

The forth ingredient is to **risk**-each of the six basic haircuts taught in this book. Soon you will become familiar with each of the six basic haircuts and be combining and altering them to create various styles. For example the same haircut can be changed by parting the hair on either side, or parted in the middle. It can be combed forward or pulled back off the face, sculpted, gelled, blow dried or left natural. Sideburns can be left long, medium, short, angled, straight or softly rounded. Perming and highlighting can give hair the personality and texture needed for achieving the look you want.

Before starting the haircutting process, you will need to take a realistic look at the child's hair you are about to cut. The child will be referred to in the feminine gender throughout the book with the exception of the section on shorter haircuts where the masculine gender will be used.

Take the time to discuss what hair style your child wants. The most common complaint I've heard is "She didn't cut my hair the way I wanted it cut".

Communication is the key to successful haircutting. Take the time to listen, to what your child wants and repeat what you heard her say. Do this until you have a clear picture of your child's desired hairstyle crystalized in your mind. Some helpful questions to ask might be how much length do you want taken off? Do you like a part? If so where? Do you want bangs? If so how much? How long? Do you like wearing your hair forward or back off your face? Do you want a clean blunt line to your cut or a soft wispy look? How much ear do you want exposed?

If your child needs your help on deciding what hairstyle would be best suited for their type of hair, consider their head and facial shape as well as their hair texture.

Head and facial shapes

In helping your child choose her hair style, you want to choose a cut that will give her face the appearance of being perfectly oval. This can be done by adding width to a narrower face and adding height to a wider face. To give the appearance of more width, use medium to long bangs with chin length hair or shorter. Longer layers also give the illusion of having thick, full ends which makes the narrower face appear wider.

Height can be added by cutting short layers at the crown. Either very short hair or shoulder length and longer will enhance the wider face. Never draw attention to the areas of width by having the finished length end at the point of greatest width. This will only emphasize the width that you are trying to camouflage. You want to draw attention to other areas to minimize the appearance of width.

Narrow Face

Right   Wrong

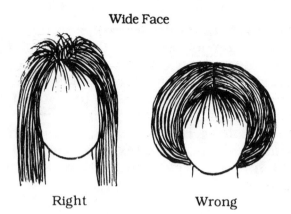

Wide Face

Right   Wrong

Types of hair

There are many textures and types of hair thick, medium, thin, curly, wavy, straight, coarse, medium and fine. Most hair can be cut by simply following the directions in this book. Here are a few helpful suggestions for problems you might encounter.

Straight, fine hair

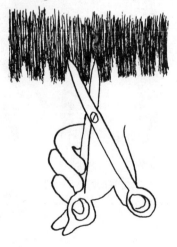

When you cut fine, straight hair, choppy cutting lines are often left in the hair. Tiny, steep, triangle shaped slivers can be cut into the very ends of the child's hair to break up these harsh lines.

Curly hair

Curly hair has the tendency to shrink when it is dry. The tighter the curl, the more shrinkage will result when the hair is dry. To compensate for this loss in length, leave the hair a little bit longer than you think you'll need.

Thick hair

Sometimes when cutting thick or coarse hair you will find your scissors unable to easily cut through the thickness. Take the hair down in sections to accommodate the amount of hair instead of trying to cut it all at one time.

Wavy hair

Wavy hair is the easiest and most forgiving hair to cut. The soft, natural curvature will hide most slight imperfections. Just follow the directions.

Now you are ready to begin the haircutting process. First, begin by reading the entire book from beginning to end. This will familiarize you with the contents of the book. At the beginning of each haircut, always start with chapters 1 through 6. These chapters describe the steps used at the start of each haircut. The six basic haircuts are found in chapters 7 through 12. If none of these haircuts will work for your child, read chapters 13 and 14. These chapters discuss combining and/or altering the six basic cuts to create most any style.

Chapter 15 lightly touches upon the techniques of blow drying and using the curl iron to style your finished cut. Perming and highlighting are discussed in chapters 16 and 17. These chemical services can give hair that texture or character sometimes needed for the finished look.

The purpose of this book is to teach the art of haircutting not to just memorize haircuts. If you combine the knowledge you learn from this book with experience and your own creativity, you will be able to cut just about anyone's hair with confidence.

1
The Tools

In order to cut hair well, you will need a small assortment of tools. This ensemble consists of a pair of ice-tempered, stainless steel, haircutting scissors, a plastic all purpose comb marked in inches, a waterproof cape, a spray bottle, a neck brush and five plastic or metal hair clips. **You can order an inexpensive quality kit that contains these tools by filling out and sending the order form at the back of this book**. Another place these tools may be individually purchased, is at your local beauty or barber supply. A small investment in quality tools will make haircutting a much more enjoyable learning experience.

Scissors

A pair of 5 inch, ice-tempered, stainless steel, haircutting scissors with a finger tang. This is the most important tool for precision haircutting.

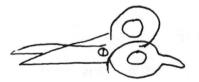

Comb

A 7 inch, plastic comb marked in inches for the purpose of measuring and comparing hair lengths throughout the cut.

Cape

A large piece of waterproof material that fastens at the back of the neck to protect the child from pieces of cut hair.

Spray Bottle

A plastic mister or spritzer used to keep the hair wet throughout the haircut.

Neck Duster

This is used to quickly and easily remove pieces of cut hair that tend to cling to the child's face, neck and clothes. It will lessen the possibility of itching and discomfort that can be caused by these hairs.

Clamps or Clips

5 plastic butterfly clamps or 5 long, thin, metal clips will assist by keeping unwanted hair up and out of the way.

(Extra optional tools)

Apron

A piece of water re-sistant material that fastens at the neck and waist is used to protect the stylist from pieces of cut hair as well as chem-icals such as perm solution, bleach, per-oxide and tint.

Razor

An electric or battery operated shaving razor with a trimming edge. This is used to remove excess neck, side burn and moustache hair. There is an alternative method using scissors, taught in chapter 14.

Thinning shears

These are shears used to take out unwanted bulk and thickness in the child's hair. An alternative method of thinning hair using scissors is also taught in chapter 14.

Blowdryer and curling iron

A blow dryer and curling iron are the tools usually used to style and complete the finished haircut.

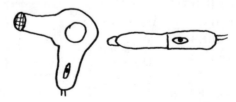

2
The Shop Set-up

You don't need to spend too much time and energy worrying about where to set up shop. Just about any place will do. I've cut hair in almost every room in the house.

The bathroom seems to lend itself well to

haircutting. A large mirror, good lighting, an easy to clean floor, and a convenient counter top where tools can easily be reached makes haircutting an easier and much more enjoyable experience.

3
To Start

Start by thoroughly brushing the hair. This will loosen any dry scalp flakes and bring the natural oils from the scalp to the ends. The bristles will help to massage the scalp and stimulate good blood circulation as well as eliminate snarls.

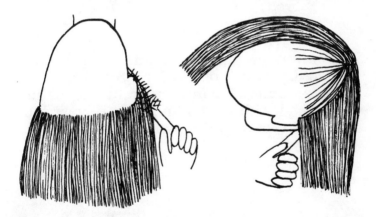

After a good brushing, always start by shampooing the child's hair. This will make the hair more manageable and pliable. Apply a small amount of shampoo, massage well and rinse until the hair is suds free. Now rinse the hair one last time with cold water. The cold water will help remove any lingering trace of shampoo and eliminate any dull film or residue. Cold water causes the cuticle or outermost layer of the hair to close, creating a flat surface like a mirror. The hair will reflect light and have a brilliant sheen as well as be protected from most harmful elements.

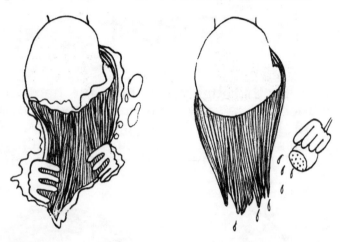

A conditioner may be applied if the child's hair is dry or full of tangles. Squeeze a moderate amount of conditioner in the palm of your hand, rub your hands together and distribute it evenly to the hair shafts.

Now rinse the hair with tepid water. Rinse one last time with cold water to give the hair shine and towel dry the hair.

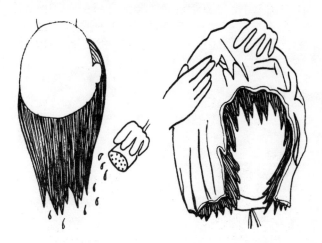

Handywork

Learning to hold and manipulate the scissors and comb comes with practice. At first it may seem awkward, but don't get discouraged. Soon it will be second nature. Be sure to take the time to read and practice this "handy work" before going any further.

How to hold scissors

Begin by placing the thumb of your most dexterous hand through the large hole and your ring finger through the small hole of the scissors. Rest your pinky on the finger tang. The scissors will stay in this hand while the comb will continually change hands.

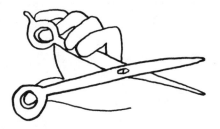

Holding the comb

Slip just your thumb from the large scissor hole. Now lay your scissors in the palm of your hand.

Place the comb in that same hand (now holding the scissors) between the index finger and thumb. Now comb the child's hair with the wide tooth end of the comb.

With your free hand, grasp the childs hair, between the index and middle fingers. Slide the fingers down the hair shaft applying pressure to create tension. Fingers should stop sliding just above the point at which the hair will be cut.

Comb exchange

While still holding the hair between the index and middle fingers of your less dexterous hand, place the comb in that same hand, between the thumb and index finger.

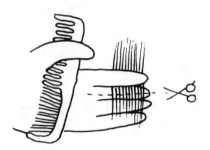

Cutting

Place the thumb of your more dexterous hand back through the large hole of the scissors. You will cut the hair just beneath the index and middle fingers holding the hair. Use these fingers as a straight edge and cut parallel to them.

5
Bangs

If bangs are not necessary for your particular haircut, you may skip over this chapter.

There are three types of bangs: light, medium and heavy. They range from a sheer bang to a full bang.

To create bangs you will be using a semi-circle part which extends from one temple to the other. The more shallow semi-circle creates fewer bangs, while the deeper semi-circle creates fuller bangs.

Decide from the following pictures how much bangs are desired.

| Light | Medium | Heavy |

Once this decision has been made, part the hair in a semi-circle accordingly. This parting will separate the bang hair from the rest of the hair. Comb the remaining hair away from the child's face and clip it up, out of the way. This will help define the bang section.

Top View

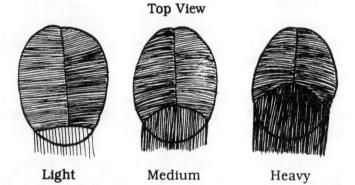

Light   Medium   Heavy

Towel dry as much moisture out of the bang section as possible to achieve a natural, dry bang length.

Comb the bang hair directly forward, laying the wet hair flat against the child's forehead so it sticks to the skin.

Decide upon the length and the contour of the bangs.

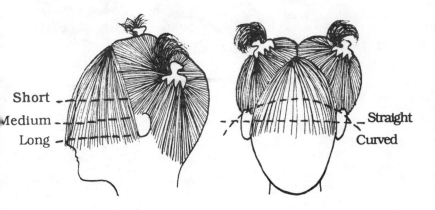

Short
Medium
Long

Straight
Curved

Do you want a soft curved line or a straight blunt line?

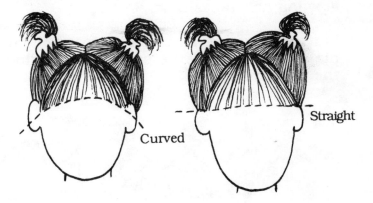

Curved

Straight

Use the distance between the bridge and the tip of the child's nose as a measuring tape. Cutting closer to the bridge creates shorter bang lengths while cutting closer to the tip creates longer bangs.

Short   Medium   Long

Remember wet hair will shrink when it is dry. The most common complaint is, "My bangs are too short!", so when in doubt as far as establishing length, leave a little bit more length than you think you'll need. It just takes a few minutes to cut more length, but growing hair takes time.

Start cutting wet, flattened bangs at one temple moving toward the center and ending at the other temple.

Cut the entire bang section to the desired amount, curve and length. If no layering is desired, the bangs are finished. **If layers are wanted go on**.

Layered bangs have more fullness than blunt, or unlayered bangs. This is because the bangs have less weight. Feathering is another term used for layering bangs. If layers are desired take the <u>entire</u> bang section between the index and middle fingers of your less dexterous hand. Pull the hair up to the desired horizontal angle needed for the amount of layering wanted.

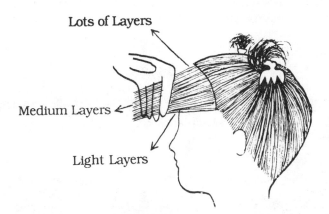

Hold the hair tautly at this angle while sliding your fingers down the hair shafts until the underneath hairs begin to fall from your fingers on to the forehead. Still holding the hair at the same angle, cut the bangs parallel to your fingers. The higher the angle you hold the bangs, the more layering will result.

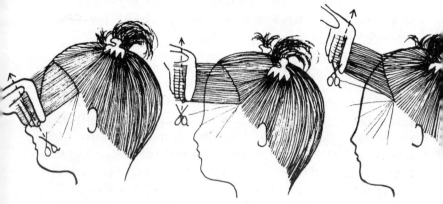

Light Layers   Medium Layers   Lots of Lay

Now that the bangs have been cut, you may begin "Creating the Outline"

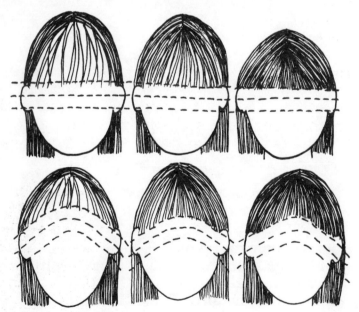

Creating the Outline
6

With the exception of the "ALL ONE LENGTH" CUT, "Creating the Outline" is the foundation on which the rest of the haircuts are built. It defines the shape and outline of the entire cut. Hair will be cut around the child's face, neck and ears to the varied lengths needed to outline your individual haircut.

Read and follow the directions for chapters 1-5. The hair should be washed and lightly towel dried. The bangs should already be cut. Be sure your child's head is held erect and facing forward to insure symmetry.

Using the crown as a pivot point. Comb the child's hair directly down from the crown laying the wet hair flat against her face, neck and ears so that it sticks to her skin.

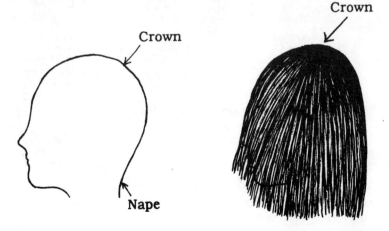

Crown

Crown

Nape

Look at the following pictures. Choose the outline that most closely defines the child's desired haircut.

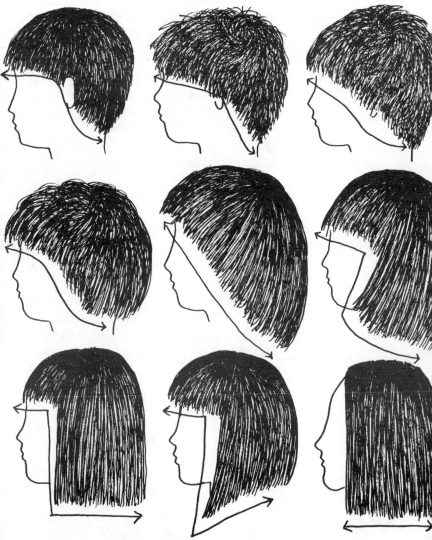

Stand in front of the child. Notice that you can see the "cut bang" hair length. You should be able to see the cut bangs through the long hairs laying over them. Cut these long hairs to the same length and curve as the cut bangs beneath.

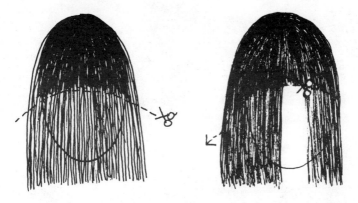

Sometimes when cutting thick or coarse hair you will find your scissor unable to easily cut through the thickness. Take the hair down in sections to accommodate the amount of hair instead of trying to cut it all at one time.

Stand in back of the child. Ask her to show you with her hand the exact length that she would like her hair in the back to be cut.

Cut a 2" wide section of nape hair directly at the center back of the head to the desired length for the back hair.

You will complete this outline by connecting both the front and back cut lengths. This can be done by cutting both sides of the child's hair.

Stand directly in front of the child. Begin on the child's right side. Use the bang length as a guide for cutting the hair laying on top of and beside it. Cut the hair from the front to the back. The side hairs should be cut to the necessary lengths to create the outline of your individual cut.

When cutting hair <u>over</u> the ears, take care
not to nip the ear. Press the ear flat against
the child's head with your less dexterous
hand while cutting.

If you are cutting hair <u>around</u> the ears, press
each ear forward with your less dexterous
hand while cutting the hair.

Stand in back of the child.   Begin on the

child's left side. Cut from the back to front. The hair should be cut to the necessary lengths to create the outline of your individual cut. Use the bang length as a guide for cutting the hair laying on top of and beside it at the completion of this step.

When the entire outline has been cut make sure the child's head is erect and facing forward. To be sure that both sides of your cut are identical, stand directly in front of the child at eye level. Take a pinch of hair from the same place on both sides and pull them tautly to compare length.

If you are unsure by feel you can also use the

measurements on your comb to help compare lengths. If evening is needed, cut just a little length at a time from the longer side until both sides are even.

Comb her hair straight down from the crown with the wide tooth end of the comb. Cut any uneven hairs.

Now comb the child's hair straight down from the crown using the **fine tooth end** of the comb. Cut stray or uneven hairs.

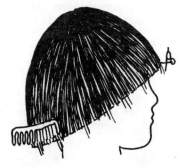

You are now ready to begin the haircut of your choice.

7
Cut 1

All-One-length cut

The first cut is called the all-one-length haircut because all of the hairs are cut to the exact same length causing the ends to form a straight blunt edge.

Read and follow the directions in chapters 1-5. **(There is no need to create the outline for this haircut.)** The hair should be freshly washed and lightly towel dried. Remember, if bangs are desired for the child's hairstyle, they should be cut before beginning this haircut.

Part your child's hair where she desires. If no part is wanted, part her hair down the middle to create symmetry.

Be sure the child's head is held erect and facing forward throughout the haircut. This will insure symmetry.

Comb the child's hair straight down using the wide tooth end of the comb. Cut a few strands in the very front of the child's left side to the desired length. Remember wet hair will shrink when it is dry.

Now do the same with a few strands from the

very front of the child's right side so that the cut lengths on both sides match.

Check to be sure that both sides are even by standing directly in front of the child at eye level. Take a pinch of cut hair from both sides and pull them tautly to see if both sides are the same length. If evening is needed, cut off just a little length at a time from the longer side until the two sides are even and at the desired length. These cut hairs will serve as a guide for length throughout the rest of the haircut.

To complete this haircut you want to connect both of the cut side lengths by cutting the back.

Start by using the cut hair on the child's right side as a guide to match the hair laying beside it in length. Using your handy work comb the hair on the child's right side of the head straight down. Cut the hair beside the pre-cut hair to the identical length. Remember to keep the child's head straight forward and erect throughout the cut.

Now move slightly to the child's left.

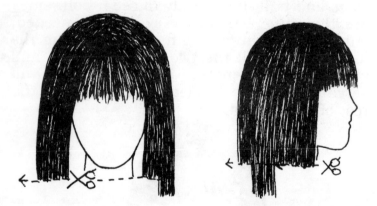

Sometimes when cutting thick or coarse hair you will find your scissors unable to easily cut through the thickness. Take the hair down in sections to accommodate the amount of

hair instead of trying to cut it all at one time.

Repeat the last step **(written in bold)** moving slowly from the child's right side to her left side until you meet the pre-cut strands of hair on the left side. All the hair should now be the same length.

49

Comb the hair straight down using the **wide tooth end** of the comb. Cut any uneven hairs to create a clean, sharp line.

To check your haircut be sure the child's head is erect and facing forward. Comb the child's hair straight down with the **fine tooth end** of the comb. Cut any stray hairs you might have missed to sharpen the blunt edge and complete the finished "all-one-length" cut.

Now the hair is ready to be styled.

8

Cut 2

Undercut

This haircut is often referred to as "the bob" or "page boy" cut. The underneath hairs are cut to a shorter length than the top or surface hairs. This graduation from shorter to longer lengths will cause the ends of the hair to softly curl under toward the face. This particular haircut will take some work on the child's part to respond to your gently pushing her head and neck in different positions.

Read and follow the directions for chapters 1-6. Bangs should be cut and the outline created before beginning this hair cut.

To create the shorter underneath hair length, stand in back and push the child's

51

head completely forward until her chin rests on her collar bone. Comb the hair with the wide tooth end of the comb laying it flat against the back of her head and bent neck so that it sticks to the skin. Using the flat side of your less dexterous hand, flatten the child's hair against her neck.

You will notice that the nape hairs underneath are slightly longer than the surface hairs. Cut the underneath hair in the back to the identical length of the surface hair.

Stand on the child's right side and press her head all the way to her left side until her left ear is resting on her left shoulder. Comb and press the wet hair flat against the right side of the child's face and neck so that the hair sticks to the skin. Again you will notice that the underneath hairs are a bit longer than the surface hairs. Continue to cut the underneath hair on her right side to the same length as the top or surface hair.

Stand on the child's left side and press the child's head all the way to her right side until her right ear is resting on her right shoulder. Comb and press the wet hair flat against the left side of the child's face and neck so that it sticks to the skin. Cut the longer underneath hair to the exact length as the surface hair on the left side. After cutting the entire head of hair, check to be sure no hairs have been missed.

To check this haircut, roll the head slowly from the child's right, then forward and to her left constantly combing the hair flat against the head and neck with the **fine tooth end** of the comb. Cut off any long or uneven stray hairs to the same length as the rest of the hair.

Now the hair is ready to be styled.

9
Cut 3

Beveled Cut

The beveled cut is a slightly layered haircut. Layers are a result of hair being elevated while being cut. The ends have less weight which creates a softer and fuller effect.

Read and follow the directions for chapters 1-6. The bangs should be cut and the outline created before beginning this haircut.

Study the pictures below and decide how much layering the child desires for her hairstyle. This will determine at what angle or elevation the hair should be held while being cut.

Stand on the child's right side. The child's head should be held erect and facing straight forward. Take a small (about 2 1/2" wide) section of hair between the index and middle fingers of your less dexterous hand. Hold the section of hair tautly at the angle chosen. The higher the hair is elevated, the more layering will result as shown in the last diagram.

Holding the hair at that elevation, slowly slide the fingers down the hair shafts until the underneath hairs begin to lightly fall from your fingers. (The underneath hairs that have fallen do not need to be cut. Their length has already been established while creating the outline.)

Stop sliding at this point. Cut the rest of the hair still being held between your index and middle fingers in a horizontal line. Cut at the point at which you can see the already cut shorter lengths beneath the longer surface hairs. The ends will appear to be a bit thinner. Cut these thinner hairs in a parallel line just beneath your fingers using them as a straight edge. Let the section of hair fall from your fingers.

Move slightly to the child's left.

Use the cut hair as a guide for length. Take one half (approximately 1" wide) section of the "just cut" hair along with a small (approximately 2" wide) section of uncut hair beside it. Hold the section of hair tautly between the index and middle fingers of your less dexterous hand at the exact same angle as you held the last section.

Keeping the hair at this angle, slide your fingers down the hair shafts until the underneath hairs begin to fall from your grasp. Stop sliding at this point.

Make a horizontal cut in the section of elevated hair just below your index and middle fingers, using them as a straight edge to cut along.

Repeat the last step **(written in bold)** moving a little to the child's left each time until the entire head of hair is cut.

To check this haircut, take 2 1/2" wide sections of hair and hold them <u>vertically</u> between the index and middle fingers of your less dexterous hand. The ends should form a straight line following the same vertical angle as the arrows on the diagram indicate for the various amount of layering desired. Cut any stray hairs that stick out from this vertical line.

Now the hair is ready to be styled.

10
CUT

long layered cut

This hair cut creates lots of layers on top, while leaving most of the weight and length at the bottom. These layers give height and fullness to long hair.

Read and follow directions for chapters 1-6. The bangs should be cut and the outline created before beginning this haircut.

Hold a few strands of hair from the top of the child's head straight up. Ask the child to

show you with her fingers exactly how short
she wants the layers to be on top.

Measure the strands of hair from the child's
scalp to her fingers with the measurements
on the comb. This will be the determining
length at which the hair will be cut.

Stand in front of the child. Have the child stand up and bend forward at the waist. Her head should be totally upside down. Using the wide tooth end of the comb, comb her hair directly overhead. Be sure the child's hair is free of tangles and in an orderly fashion in the upside down position.

Hold the comb at the base of the scalp on the crown. Use the measurements on the comb to indicate exactly where the desired layer length should be cut.

Grasp the entire head of hair at that measured point between the index and middle fingers of your less dexterous hand.

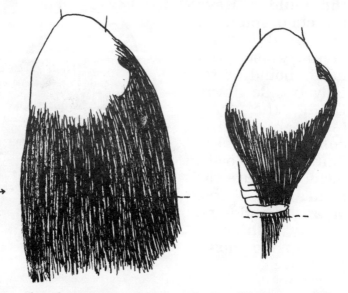

Cut the hair just below these fingers. (The nape hairs do not need to be cut since their length has already been established when you "created the outline".) The closer to the scalp you cut the child's hair, the shorter the layers will be.

Bring the child to the upright position. Cut again any long, stray hairs along the outline of the haircut.

Now the hair is ready to be styled.

Cut 5

Medium layered cut

The medium layered cut is for a girl's shorter hairstyle or a boy's long to medium length hairstyle. The hair is cut to the same length all over the head.

Read and follow the directions for chapters 1-6. The bangs should be cut and the outline created before beginning this haircut.

Hold a few strands of hair at the top (crown) of the child's head straight up. Ask the child to show you with her fingers how short she wants her layers to be.

Measure the strands of hair from the child's scalp to her fingers with the measurements on the comb.

Cut those strands of hair just above her fingers. This will be the determining length at which the rest of the hair will be cut.

Picture the child's head as a peeled orange with all of the sections exposed. Start at the crown and work your way to the nape.

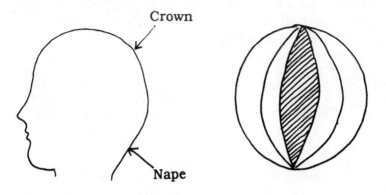

Crown

Nape

Stand in back of the child. Grasp the crown hairs of the back orange section, between the index and middle fingers of your less dexterous hand. The fingers should be positioned <u>vertically</u> at the desired layer length. Cut just above your fingers allowing their contour to be your guide for the cutting line. Start at

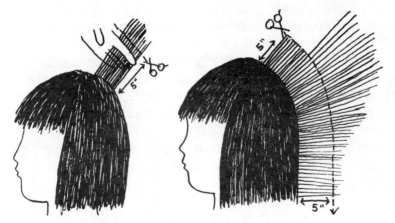

the crown and rember to work down the orange section to the nape.

Move to the next "orange section" on the child's right. Start at the crown and work your way to the nape.

Take a small amount of "just cut" hair (approximately 1/2 " wide section) along with the new 2" wide section of hair. The cut hair will serve as a guide for the cutting length. Hold this vertical section of hair tautly between the index and middle fingers of your less dexterous hand. The fingers should be positioned vertically at the desired layer length. Cut just above your fingers allowing their contour to be your guide for the cutting line.

Repeat the last step **(written in bold)** moving slowly from the back, section by section all the way to the child's right.

Repeat the same step **(written in bold)** moving slowly from the back, section by section, all the way to the child's left.

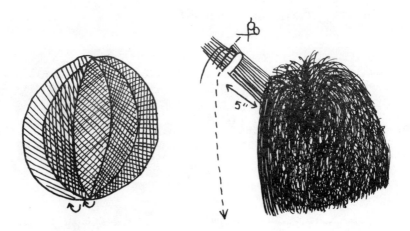

Cut any stray hairs to neaten and define the outline of the finished cut.

Now check your hair cut to be sure every hair is the same length. Picture the child's hair as a corn field. No matter which way you look down the corn rows, (front, side or diagonal) the rows form straight lines. The child's hair should be the same length all over no matter which direction you pull it.

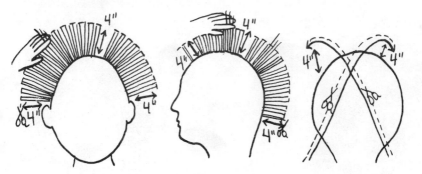

The haircut is now complete and ready to be styled.

12

Cut 6

Short layered cut

This very short layer cut is often referred to as the shingled or tapered cut. This method can be used just at the nape of the neck, over the ears, or over the entire head. A whole head of hair cut in this method will result in a butch or crew cut. The effect is similar to that of an electric razor cut given at a barber shop.

Read and follow the directions for chapters 1-6. The bangs should be cut and the outline created before beginning this hair cut.

Visualize the child's head as a peeled orange with the sections exposed. Begin at the center section in the back of the child's head.

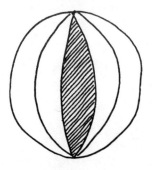

The thickness of the comb will be the determining length at which the child's hair will be cut. The end of the comb with the wider teeth is usually used unless the child wants a shorter length. If this is the case, use the small tooth end of the comb. If a longer length is desired, use your finger depth in place of the comb.

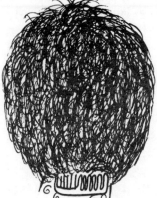

Stand in back of the child. Begin at the base of the child's neck with the nape hair. Hold the **fine tooth end** of the comb with your less dexterous hand laying the **wide tooth end** flat against the child's neck. The teeth should be facing upward just below his hairline.

Slowly move the flattened, wide tooth end of the comb up the center orange section in the back of the child's head. The comb will serve as a rake. Cut the hairs as they stick through between the wide teeth of the flattened comb. The cuts will be made just above the comb so that the thickness of the comb is your guide for length. Work from the bottom to the top of that center orange section in the back of the head until it is completed. Now move one section to the child's right.

Holding the fine tooth end place the comb flat against the child's neck with the wide teeth facing upward just below the hairline. Move the comb slowly up this orange section cutting the raked hairs as they stick out between the teeth. Work from the bottom to the top until this orange section is completed. Move one more section to the child's right.

Continue to rake and cut the hair starting at the bottom of each section and working your way up to the top of the child's head until you've completed the right side.

Now do the same procedure starting at the back. Work toward the child's left side until the entire left side of the child's hair has been cut.

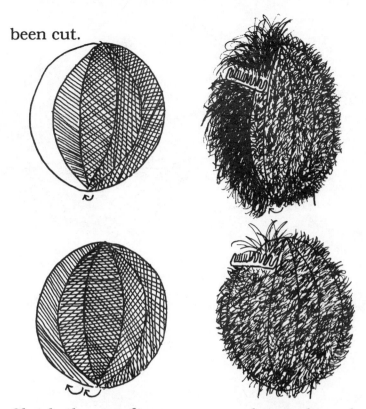

Check the cut for uneven or choppy lines by raking the hair in an upward direction from front to back, side to side and diagonally with the wide tooth end of the comb, cut any uneven hairs to create a uniform length.

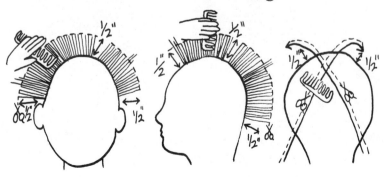

Now the hair is ready to be styled.

neck hairs. If you don't have an electric razor this method can be used.

Push the child's head all the way forward. This will stretch the skin and give it tension so that there are no folds or creases of loose skin that can accidentally be nipped.

Hold the scissors in your more dexterous hand, laying them flat against the child's neck. Continually glide the scissors open and closed while sliding them along his neck. Always keep the scissors parallel to the neck to keep the tips of the scissors from nipping the skin. Do this until all unsightly neck hairs are gone.

Cowlicks, Widow's peaks and Whirls

Cowlicks

A cluster of hair that sticks up because of the different directions the hair grows from the scalp. They are often located in the front.

Widow's Peaks

A bunch of hair that forms a peak or V shape. They are usually found at the hairline in front or at the nape of the neck.

Whirls

A group of hair that grows in a circular pattern or spinning wheel fashion. They are usually found in the crown area.

Cowlicks, widow's peaks and whirls can be treated by leaving length which adds weight to these problem hairs that stick up, so that they lay down.

Breaking up the "Chop lines"

Chop lines are unnatural looking cut marks left by scissors in the hair. They appear most often when cutting straight, fine, blond hair. To camouflage these lines, cut shallow, narrow V shapes into the very ends of the hair These V shapes will break up the harsh, straight edge.

Thinning Hair

There are two ways to thin out unwanted weight or bulk in thick hair. The first way is to use thinning shears. Thinning shears look like a pair of scissors with teeth missing on one or both blades.

These shears are held and used like haircutting scissors. The shears should be held at various angles approximately 3" from the child's scalp. The angle at which the thinning shears are held should constantly change. Thinning should be confined to the bulky areas only and used sparingly so as to avoid creating "holes".

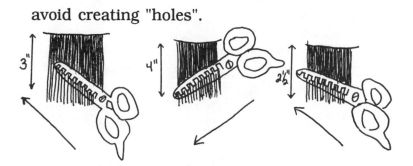

A second way to thin hair (using regular scissors), is to vertically cut deep, narrow V shapes into the child's hair. This can thin out the hair giving it a similar effect as the thinning shears without having to invest in another tool. Again thinning should be used in only the bulky or thicker areas to avoid creating holes in your cut.

14
Combinations

Combinations should be attempted only after you feel comfortable with each of the six basic haircuts. All of the following hairstyles and more can be created by simply combining two or more of the six basic haircuts and giving them a twist.

Each of the illustrated combinations give a front, side and back view of the hairstyle. The combinations are broken down into four categories: outline (chapter 6), bangs (chapter 5), haircut(s) that are combined (each are separate chapters 7-11) and alterations (chapter 12).

Remember, even the same haircut can look different by just parting the hair on either side or down the middle, combing it forward or pulling it back off the face. Hair can be sculpted, blowdryed, gelled or left natural. By simply combining the knowledge found in this book with your own creativity, you can cut just about any hairstyle imaginable.

Outline: 9   **Bangs:** none   **Cuts:** cut 1

Outline: 4   **Bangs:** Medium   **Cuts:** cut 1

Outline: 5   **Bangs:** none   **Cuts:** cut 2

Outline: 5 **Bangs:** Medium **Cuts:** cut 2

Outline: 8 **Bangs:** none **Cuts:** cut 2

Outline: 8 **Bangs:** heavy **Cuts:** cut 2

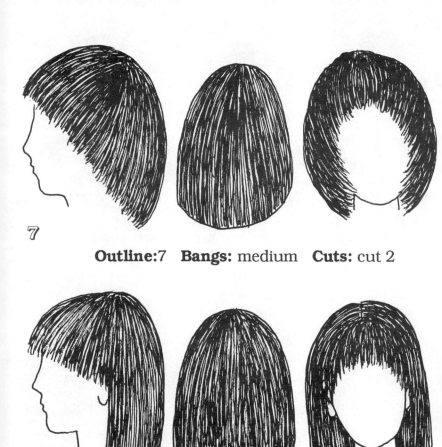

Outline: 7   **Bangs:** medium   **Cuts:** cut 2

Outline: 4   **Bangs:** heavy   **Cuts:** cut 1

Outline: 8   **Bangs:** medium   **Cuts:** cut 2

90

Outline: 8-right 5-left **Bangs:** none **Cuts:** cut 2

Outline: 8 **Bangs:** heavy **Cuts:** cut 1-front, cut 3-sides

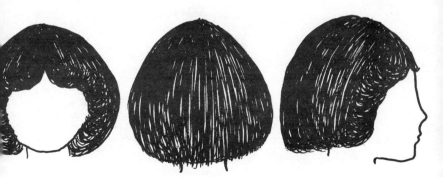

Outline:7 **Bangs:** medium **Cuts:** cut 3-front and sides
cut 2-back

Outline: 7 **Bangs:** light **Cuts:** cut 1

Outline: 8-right 5-left **Bangs:** none **Cuts:** cut 1

Outline: 7 **Bangs:** heavy **Cuts:** cut 4

Outline: 7 **Bangs:** medium **Cuts:** cut 4

Outline: 7 **Bangs:** light **Cuts:** cut 2-back, cut 3-sides

Outline: 2-lower Nape **Bangs:** medium **Cuts:** 5-front
and sides, cut 6 back, cut 3 rest
Alterations: dovetail neckline 93

19

Outline: 7   **Bangs:** medium   **Cuts:** cut 3

20

Outline: 7   **Bangs:** heavy   **Cuts:** cut 3

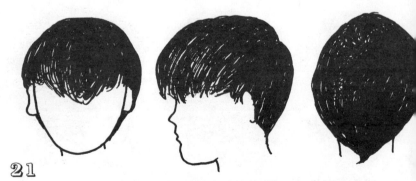

21

Outline: 1   **Bangs:** heavy   **Cuts:** cut 5
Alterations: dovetail neckline

94

Outline: 1 **Bangs:** heavy **Cuts:** cut 5
Alterations: round neckline, short square sideburns

Outline: 2 **Bangs:** heavy **Cuts:** cut 5
Alterations: dovetail neckline, short slanted sideburns

Outline: 7 **Bangs:** medium **Cuts:** cut 5
Alterations: cut "V" shapes into ends of hair

95

Outline: 3 **Bangs:** medium **Cuts:** cut 5
Alterations: square neckline, "V" shapes cut into ha
ends

Outline: 1 **Bangs:** medium **Cuts:** cut 5
Alterations: square neckline, medium angled sidebu

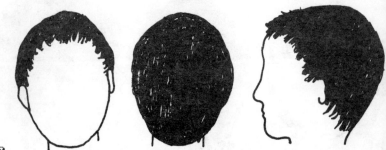

Outline: 2 **Bangs:** medium **Cuts:** cut 5
Alterations: round neckline, short slanted sideburn
96   "V" shapes cut into ends of hair

8

Outline: 1   **Bangs:** medium   **Cuts:** cut 6
Alterations: square neckline, medium slanted sideburns, leave length at corners to create square edges

9

Outline: 1   **Bangs:** medium   **Cuts:** cut 6
Alterations: oval neckline, short slanted sideburns

15
Styling Tips

Blow drying

Towel dry as much wetness out of the hair as possible leaving the hair damp.

Have the child bend forward at the waist. Her head should be tipped completely upside down letting the hair dangle freely.

Blow dry the child's hair in this upside down position until the hair is barely damp and almost dry.

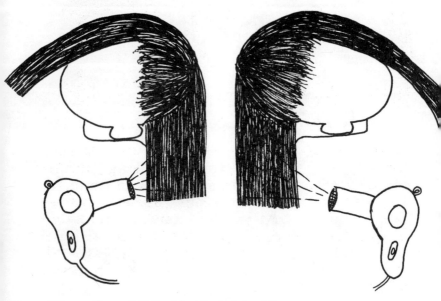

Have the child stand right side up again.

Have the child part her own hair where she

desires.

At this point apply any styling aid such as gel, mousse, lotion, or wave set. These products are used to give body and add extra texture to the hair for a longer holding style. This is done by applying a small amount to the palm of your hand, rubbing your hands together and distributing it evenly to the child's hair. If the child prefers, the hair may be left natural without any styling aid.

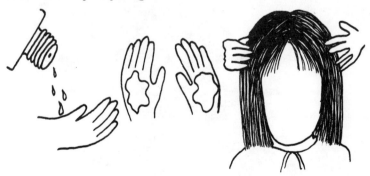

Part the child's hair down the back dividing her hair into two sections. One on either side. Clip these sections up and out of the way leaving a third of the underneath hair down. When the underneath hair is dry it will give the style a foundation for more volume, fullness and shape.

Dry the bottom third of hair starting at the roots and working toward the ends. Give direction to the hair by using a brush, comb or your fingers.

When the bottom third of the child's hair is dry, take the middle third of hair down from each section. Style it the same way.

When the middle third of the child's hair is dry, take the top third of hair down from each section and style it the same way. Now your style is complete unless more curl is desired.

Curl Iron

After the child's hair is completely dry, a curling iron can be used to enhance the style by adding curl. The curling iron is generally used to curl just the ends while hot rollers or curlers give curl to the entire hair shaft.

Use the curling iron sparingly. If clamped down on the ends for too long, dryness and damage may result.

Wrap the child's hair around the curling iron turning it in the direction you want the hair to curl.

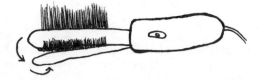

For short hair lay the comb flat on the base of the child's scalp just below the hair being curled. This will protect her scalp from being burned by the iron.

16
Perming

Materials

1 - "no heat" perm
1 - plastic cape
4 - hand towels
1 - box of "jumbo" end papers (usually includ-
ed in a non-professional perm)
Long perm rods
1 - tail comb
1 - plastic bag or shower cap

Size of rod

The smaller the rod diameter, the tighter the
curl will be. The wider the rod diameter, the
looser the curl will be. Longer rods are both
easier and quicker to use than shorter rods.

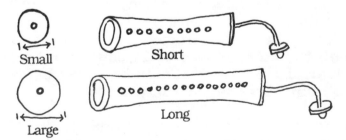

Small
Large
Short
Long

Rods come in a variety of colors:
  blue - natural or afro curl
  pink - tight curl

grey - medium curl
white - soft curl
green - tight body wave
purple - medium body wave
brown - very loose body wave
tan - texture only

First complete the child's haircut. Now using the spray bottle, wet again and lightly towel dry the child's hair.

Examine your child's scalp for any open sores. For minor sores, a generous amount of vaseline can be applied to each sore. This will help seal and protect it from the solution. **For more severe scalp conditions professional treatment should be given before beginning any chemical service.**

Make two parallel parts approximately 3 1/2" apart (or the same distance as the perm rod length) from the front to the back of the child's head. Clip the rest of the hair up and out of the way. This will create a skunk stripe right down the middle of her head.

This row will eventually be divided by horizontal partings approximately 1/2" apart (the same distance as the diameter of your perm rod) giving the appearance of railroad ties.

Stand in front of the child and start at her forehead. Wrap the very first 1/2" parting of hair forward. Clip the rest of the child's hair back out of the way. Elevate the hair to a 45 degree angle using a moderate amount of tension.

Hold the hair flat between the index and middle fingers of your less dexterous hand. Place two end papers lengthwise on either side of the flattened hair between the fingers. Be sure to extend the end papers beyond the ends of the child's hair to protect it from being bent or damaged.

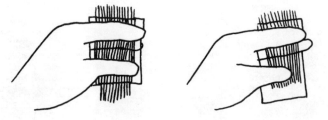

Place the perm rod beneath the end papers and roll it clockwise or under toward the scalp then fasten it.

Now stand directly behind the child. Starting at the top, just behind the first rod going forward, wrap the next 1/2" of hair the same way only now going towards the back.

Place the perm rod beneath the end papers and roll it under or clockwise toward the child's scalp. Now fasten the rod.

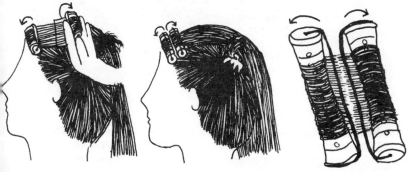

Continue to roll the hair, working from the crown to the nape until the row is finished.

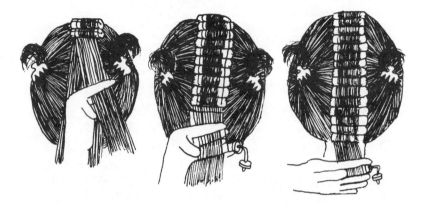

Divide each of the side sections of hair into 2 rows. The rows should each be approximately 3 1/2" wide. You should now have four rows left to be rolled.

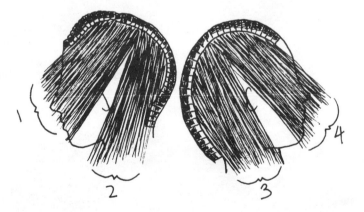

Wrap each of the four rows starting at the top and ending at the bottom. Use 1/2" sections, always rolling them clockwise or under.

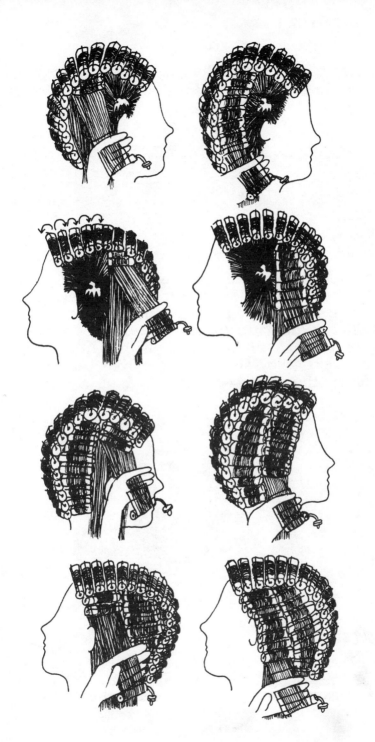

After all the child's hair is up in rods, lightly mist her hair with water.

Wrap one towel around the child's neck just beneath the plastic cape to protect her clothes. Another towel should be given to the child to hold up to her forehead for protection of her eyes and face. If the child wears contacts, they should be removed before applying the perm solution.

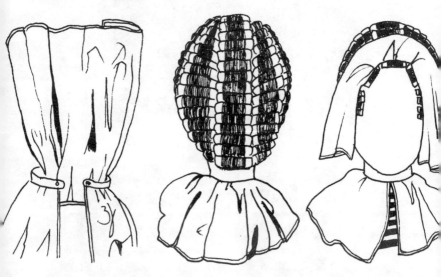

Apply the perm solution (thoroughly yet not excessively) first along the top and then along the bottom of each rod. Be sure there is enough solution to cover the entire head of rods twice.

Put a plastic bag or shower cap over the child's hair to lock in the body heat and keep the hair moist. This will help the perm to process evenly from the roots to the ends throughout the head of hair.

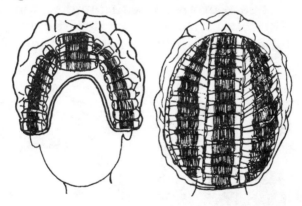

Unless the perm is pre-timed, you will need to check the curl. To do this, simply unfasten the rod and gently unwind it counter clockwise two turns. When the curve is the same size as the diameter of the perm rod being used the processing is done. Processing usually takes between 5 and 25 minutes. Timing will depend upon the porosity or resistance of the child's hair as well as the strength of the perm being used.

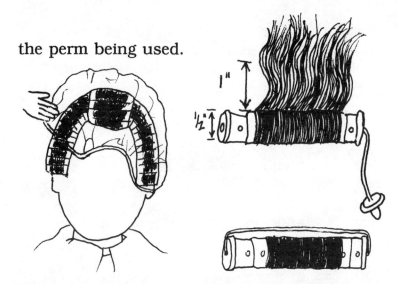

When processing is complete, rinse the hair on the rods thoroughly with tepid water for a good three minutes. Towel dry the hair by blotting it with a towel to get out the excess moisture.

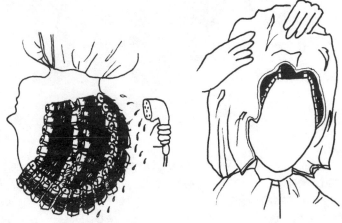

Apply the neutralizer in the same way you did the solution. **Saturate the hair thoroughly** along the top and the bottom of each perm rod. The neutralizer should be left in the hair for a full five minutes.

Remove the rods gently and quickly.

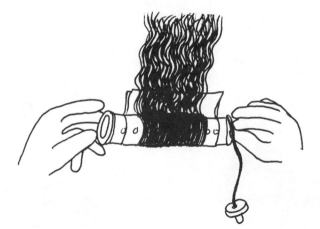

Work the neutralizer into the unwrapped hair
with your fingertips like a massage. Then

thoroughly rinse the hair.

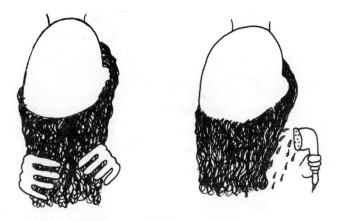

In order to rid the hair of snarls, a condition-er can be applied quickly if it is immediately rinsed out of the hair. If left on for any length of time it may loosen the perm.

Now towel dry your child's hair.

The perm is complete and the hair ready to

be styled.

17
Highlighting

Materials:

40 volume peroxide
frosting or hair bleach
a tint or painting brush
2 hand towels
plastic cape
spray bottle

Painting is the simplest and quickest method for highlighting children's hair. It will work on just about any length of hair. Keep in mind that a natural highlighting from the sun usually highlights the top or surface hairs and around the face.

Before beginning, examine your child's scalp for any sores. For minor sores apply a generous amount of vaseline to each sore. This will help protect it from the chemicals. For more severe sores professional treatment should be given before proceeding with any chemical service.

Brush your child's hair...

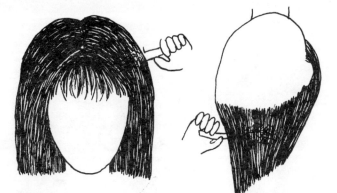

and have her part her hair where she desires.

Tuck the child's collar under...

and drape a towel around her neck. Fasten
the cape at the back of the neck and fold the
towel down.

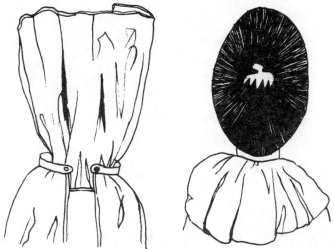

Mix equal parts of peroxide and bleach. The
mixture should be the consistency of heavy
whipped cream.

Dip your small paint or tint brush into the
mixture. Take a brush full of bleach and paint
the child's hair with long narrow strokes. You

may want a lot or very little highlights so use your own creative sense.

If the child likes to wear her hair up off the neck be sure to highlight some nape hairs at the back of her head.

Place a plastic bag snugly over the child's hair to hold in the body heat and moisture. Check the color every five minutes until the desired highlighting color has been reached.

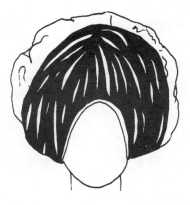

Check the color by spraying with water and lightly towel drying a few bleached strands of hair. Never leave a bleach formula on the hair for over 25 minutes or dryness and damage may result. The length of time the bleach should be left on the child's hair depends upon how light she wants her hair.

When the desired color is reached, shampoo, condition and towel dry the child's hair. The highlighting is now complete and the hair ready to be styled.